Original title:
Waves of Life's Journey

Copyright © 2025 Creative Arts Management OÜ
All rights reserved.

Author: Zachary Prescott
ISBN HARDBACK: 978-1-80587-420-1
ISBN PAPERBACK: 978-1-80587-890-2

Uncharted Waters of the Soul

In boats we float on gumball seas,
With oars made from the tallest trees.
A fish once winked; I thought it winked,
But turned out it just really stinks.

The compass spins, oh what a joke,
We navigate through clouds of smoke.
A map made by a toddler's hand,
Leads to treasures, or a band.

The seagulls laugh; they steal our fries,
While we fish for the deep-fried prize.
In pirate hats, we dance and sing,
Imaginary gold? What a thing!

So here we sail, a merry bunch,
With jellybeans for our lunch.
In uncharted depth, we'll roam and play,
For life's a game; who needs the pay?

Shores of Reflection

In flip-flops I wade, oh what a sight,
My toes in the sand, my hair a fright.
I trip on a shell, fall straight on my face,
Laughter erupts; it's my clumsy grace.

The sun's on my back, my drink spills all 'round,
Seagulls are squawking; they're poised to compound.
I wave at the kids, they throw sand at me,
And I shove it right back, it's a playful spree.

Cascading Paths

Skipping down trails, I trip on a root,
My dog gives a snicker, my foot in his boot.
He drags me along with a curious glee,
'Oh human,' he thinks, 'you're amusing, you see?'

We tumble through bushes, adventurous plight,
My coffee's now cappuccino — a mess, what a sight!
But laughter erupts like a bubbling stream,
Each stumble we take is a comic dream.

The Unseen Underneath

Beneath the smooth surface, sea creatures play,
I snorkel and splutter, losing my way.
A crab pinches gently, my scream fills the air,
It scuttles away, as if giving a dare.

I wave at the fish, who just stare with glee,
As I blow bubbles wildly, just look at me!
A turtle swims past, I'm caught in its grace,
Is it me or my antics that brighten this place?

Journey Through the Blue

Setting sail boldly, the wind in my hair,
I steer like a captain but float like a chair.
The ocean is laughing, it splashes and flips,
While I clutch at the railing, and practice my slips.

The dolphins are dancing, they tease and they twist,
I try to join in, but oh, how I missed.
With planks on the deck and a fish for a friend,
This journey is wild, but laughter won't end.

Sailing Through Shadows

In a boat made of hopes, I steer,
With a paddle of laughter, never fear.
The shadows dance, a quirky sight,
As I navigate through day and night.

A seagull squawks a joke so bold,
While my sandwich does a dance, I'm told.
With each wobble, a giggle we share,
Who knew sailing could lead to such flair?

A Journey's Horizon

As I peer at the edge of the blue,
A fish in a bowtie swims right through.
It tips its hat and winks with glee,
I think it's plotting to steal my tea.

A beacon laughs with a quirky smile,
Telling me to stay for a while.
I can't help but chuckle at the sight,
When anchors start dancing late at night.

Lost at Sea but Found

I took a wrong turn at the coral reefs,
Where jellyfish wear hats, oh what a feast!
They offered me snacks, but I politely said,
I'll stick to my chips, thanks, I'm well-fed.

A crab played chess on a driftwood scrap,
While dolphins just giggled and took a nap.
I waved to a shark, he offered a ride,
But I thought, perhaps, I'd stick to my side.

A Tidal Embrace

The tide gives a hug, a silly squish,
While I tumble and giggle, what a wish!
A starfish clapped as I fell on the sand,
Pretending it's part of my graceful land.

With seashells as friends, we start a song,
The rhythm of laughter, we hum along.
In this vast ocean, I dance with glee,
Who knew the sea could be so free?

Twilight on the Water's Edge

A fish named Fred wore a hat,
He thought he was cool, imagine that!
He danced on the shore, slipped on a rock,
While crabs all laughed, what a funny dock!

The seagulls squawked with such delight,
As Fred flailed around, what a sight!
With sand in his tail and seaweed in hair,
He waved to the crowd, 'Do I look like a bear?'

Embracing the Currents

A dolphin named Sue jumped through the air,
She claimed she could glide without a care.
But a playful wave tossed her for a spin,
And back in the water, she'd flop with a grin!

She proclaimed, 'I'm a swimmer of grace!'
Yet belly-flopped hard, what a clumsy face!
The fish held their sides, laughing so loud,
At Sue's grand entrance, she felt quite proud.

Beneath the Surface

Bubbles were rising, a party down there,
With crabs wearing shades without a care.
They danced on the sand, doing the twist,
While an octopus DJ shook his fist!

But one little shrimp couldn't keep the beat,
He slid and he slipped right onto his seat.
The crowd burst in giggles, what a silly spree,
As the shrimp grinned wide, 'It's just me being me!'

The Heart's Seabed

A clam held a secret, or so it was said,
He laughed with his friend, a soft sea snail Fred.
'If I open up wide, will I catch a gaze?'
But failed at romance in very strange ways!

The seaweed waved, trying to tease,
As Fred blushed bright, oh please, oh please!
Yet with silver laughter and shells on parade,
They danced through the tide, making quite the trade!

Shifting Sands and Soaring Dreams

In the desert, I found a sock,
Chasing mirages around the clock.
Camels laugh, with their humps so wide,
While I just trip, trying to glide.

The dunes shift, under my shoes,
Sand in my hair, like unwanted views.
With every step, I grab a bite,
Of peanut butter under the sunlight.

Kites are flying, paired with laughter,
Chasing clouds, that's what I'm after.
But the wind takes my hat, oh dear!
Guess it's a hat-free day, I cheer!

So let's traverse this golden land,
With jelly-filled pockets, oh so grand.
While comrades tumble, roll, and dance,
We stumble forward, in a merry prance.

The Undercurrent of Existence

In the pool, I splash like a fish,
Making waves with each silly swish.
Noodles float, in aquatic fun,
While I try out my latest run.

Underwater, it's a squeaky song,
Bubbles rise, and I hold on strong.
My friends wave back, looking quite absurd,
Turning each plunge into the unheard.

The lifeguard yawns, disinterested stare,
While I transform into a mermaid rare.
With fins made of pool noodles, what a sight,
A creature of joy, in the afternoon light!

Diving deep, I discover my fate,
Finding lost toys, oh isn't it great?
Let's have a splash-off, challenge the breeze,
Life's an adventure, with giggles and ease.

Horizons of Hope

Looking out at the ocean's light,
Seagulls plot their aerial flight.
I wave back with my cheesy grin,
As a wave sneaks up, and pulls me in!

Footprints in sand, leading astray,
Seashells giggle, thank you, they say.
I chatter away with seaweed weeds,
As they whisper tales of friendship and seeds.

Buckets and shovels scatter about,
Building dreams, what it's all about!
With castles that wobble, and moats of foam,
A kingdom of chaos, our sandy home!

With every crash, and retreating tide,
I leap and laugh, with worms as my guide.
So, here I stand, shovel raised high,
In the embracement of jellyfish sky!

Cresting Moments

Belly flop contests, flying through air,
With snacks in my pocket—life's not so rare!
Each tumble from a board, such a blast,
As I land in the surf, not quite so fast.

Seashells clink, like cash in a jar,
Collecting sandy memories from afar.
I scoff at the tide, come at me bro,
With a squirt gun ready, I'm set to go!

High fives exchanged, chasing each wave,
Where laughter and mischief are all but brave.
With surfboards jostling, a comedic display,
Each wipe-out a story, at the end of the day.

Sunset sinking, hues of orange and pink,
We toast with coconuts, and bubble drink.
So let's surf through life, with a grin so wide,
With every cresting moment, we take in stride.

The Driftwood Chronicles

Once I was a log, floating wide,
Chasing sunsets on the tide.
A seagull stole my donut treat,
Now I'm a snack for fish to meet.

Riding currents, feeling spry,
Whispers of the breeze pass by.
I wave to folks on distant shores,
While dodging jelly in funny scores.

Twisted tales beneath the foam,
In salty breezes, I call home.
Who needs a plan, just drift away,
Life's a dance, come join the sway.

With barnacles as friends, I cheer,
For every splash brings laughter near.
So grab a drink, let loose your wild,
In this driftwood life, remain a child.

Threads of the Cosmos

Stitched in space with cosmic thread,
My sock's adrift, oh where'd it tread?
Galactic whirlpools take my shoe,
I'll catch a star, perhaps a crew.

Comets zoom, I try to snag,
But miss, and spin like a tired rag.
Planetary hiccups, stardust glows,
Counting laughs as my journey flows.

A black hole's where my keys reside,
Lost in space, I laugh and glide.
While aliens chuckle at my plight,
I wave and wink, feeling quite alright.

Through solar winds, with cosmic cheer,
Every twist brings giggles near.
So join this game of dancing light,
In threads of laughter, we ignite.

Tides of Tomorrow

In a boat made of candy canes,
I navigate the jellybean lanes.
The tide brings tides of silly sounds,
Where licorice sharks spin 'round and 'round.

Yesterday's troubles, washed away,
Lollipops lead the dance today.
As gummy bears take to the sea,
I'll snack my way to liberty.

With every splash, a giggle pops,
Jumping jelly, swirling hops!
Tomorrow's forecast is sweet delight,
In sugary currents, I sail and bite.

So raise a toast to the ocean's spry,
With candy waves, we'll dance and fly!
For in the tide, with joy untold,
Our dreams are sweet, our fun is bold.

Currents of the Heart

My heart's a boat, with sails of cheese,
Drifting through love's playful breeze.
Each wave a giggle, a chuckling cheer,
As I float on hopes and dreams sincere.

With fishy friends sharing quirky tales,
We navigate through life's odd fails.
A dolphin twirls, wearing a hat,
And whispers secrets—can you believe that?

Seas of laughter, clouds of fun,
We spin and glide, our troubles shun.
In currents wild, where smiles flow,
Life's a circus, let's steal the show!

So grab your oars, don't be shy,
In this journey of jest, we'll soar high.
For where the heart pulses, there's glee,
And every moment's a jubilee!

Onward through the Surf

The ocean's teasing, oh so bright,
With flip-flops flying, what a sight!
We tumble, giggle, splash around,
In sandy spots, our joy is found.

The seagulls caw, they join our race,
Nabbed a chip, now it's their place!
With sunburned noses, we lay low,
Counting jellyfish, one, two, whoa!

The tide's a trickster, pulls us back,
Surfboards heave and then they crack.
I swear my swimsuit lost its grip,
As I perform my best belly zip!

But through the frolic, laughter flows,
We frolic as the ocean grows.
With every splash, we find our cheer,
In this vast sea, we've not a fear!

The Bridge Between Islands

A bridge of planks, it's swaying wide,
With crafty crabs we take a ride.
On each side, the waters sway,
Who thought a stroll could be this play?

A seagull perched with quite a smug,
Might steal your snack, just give a shrug!
To island hop is quite the fun,
But wait, my snack? It's now a bun!

Beneath our feet, fish dance and dart,
As we try our best to outsmart.
With every wobble, giggles ring,
Balancing acts are our new fling!

And when we reach the other shore,
We celebrate with chips galore.
From barnacle kisses to seaweed dust,
We've conquered that bridge, adventure's a must!

Essence of the Shore

The beach is calling, sun all day,
We dig in sand, come what may!
A crab scuttles by, with a cheeky grin,
In his tiny world, he's sure to win.

We build castles, tall and proud,
Waves crash down, so loud, so loud!
With moats and shells that shine like stars,
Until the tide claims our sweet avatars.

Throw sunscreen on, what a task,
Did I get my back? Don't dare to ask!
We wave to friends across the bay,
While seagulls plot to steal our bray.

But laughter reigns, as we chase the foam,
Finding mermaids, far from home.
For in this mirth, and salty air,
The shores do dance without a care!

Tidal Dreams

In slumber, I surf through a dream,
On a floaty shaped like ice cream!
The tide pulls me in, what a ride,
With dolphins leaping by my side.

They want to race, can I keep pace?
Splashing about, with such a grace!
But then I trip, oh what a sight,
Inflatable whale takes my flight!

On sandy tongues, we laugh and play,
Dodge those tides that swirl away.
I wake to echoes of seaweed tunes,
In a salty sleep, beneath the moons.

With goggle marks upon my face,
I'll ride again, just set the pace.
For dreams of tides are quite the thrill,
In this ocean of joy, we find our fill!

Embracing the Storm

When thunder claps and rain drops fall,
I wear a hat that's much too small.
A dance in puddles, splashes fly,
I laugh and shout, let's give it a try!

The wind may howl, but I don't care,
I'll twirl around like I'm a billionaire.
With every gust, I'll glide and sway,
Tomorrow's sunshine will come my way!

Umbrellas flip like crazy kites,
My soggy socks hold wild delights.
So let it storm, let it rain,
I'll be the star of this wet refrain!

In rainboots bright, I prance with glee,
A muddy masterpiece, that's just me!
With every drop, a chuckle's near,
Who knew a storm could bring such cheer?

Anchored in Solitude

In my little boat, I float alone,
With snacks galore, my favorite zone.
I wave at fish, they wink in delight,
Together we share this peaceful night.

The stars above are having a ball,
While I serenade them, feel so small.
A lonely seagull joins my tune,
He squawks back, thinking he's a cartoon.

I cast my line for a friend or two,
But it's just old boots giving me rue.
Still, I chuckle at the catch of the day,
Who needs fish when you're here to play?

With snacks all gone, I start to doze,
Dreaming of adventures on these shores I chose.
In solitude, I find my fun,
A party for one, and I've just begun!

Celestial Rhythms

The moon winks down with a giggle bright,
As stars do their twinkling, fun-filled flight.
Comets zoom, what a sight to see,
I wish they'd come down and dance with me!

Planets collision, what a mess!
Bumping and bouncing, oh the stress!
But in this chaos, there's joy, oh dear,
A cosmic party, let's grab a beer!

Shooting stars with wishes so wild,
Dreams take off, laughter unstyled.
Galactic games, a cosmic race,
Who knew the universe was such a place?

So if you find the night sky too quiet,
Remember the cosmos throws its own riot.
With every twinkle, a chuckle's shared,
Life's a hoot, and the stars have dared!

Resilience in the Riptide

I dive right in, hoping for a thrill,
But the current pulls fast; oh what a chill!
Flipping and flopping, I ride the tide,
With giggles and splashes, I'm along for the ride.

My floaty's popped; oh what a tragedy!
But I paddle harder, embracing my majesty.
With a laugh and a splat, I stumble and crash,
Like a fish on land, I flop with some flash!

The waves keep rolling, I rise and I fall,
Each splash a story, oh what a ball!
I'll learn to swim with the quirkiest flair,
Making friends with jellyfish who just don't care.

As tides may toss me to and fro,
I dance on the sea; it's all in the flow.
With every plunge, I embrace the ride,
In this kooky ocean, I'll never hide!

From Depth to Shore

Splashing around in muddy tides,
Finding treasures where the sea hides.
A fish that sings, a crab that dances,
Who knew the sea had such silly chances?

Sandcastles tall, they're bound to fall,
As seagulls caw, we laugh through it all.
With every splash, new friends arise,
Even the seaweed has its own surprise!

Jumping in puddles, oh what a sight,
Splattered and drenched, yet full of delight.
Chasing the tide as it runs afar,
Who knew the ocean was such a bazaar?

So here's to the laughs that the sea bestows,
And the silly things that each wave knows.
From sodden socks to sunburned cheeks,
These playful days are the life we seek!

As the Sea Meets the Sky

Clouds wear hats as they float on by,
The sun winks down with a golden eye.
Fish flying high, quite the odd sight,
They're just as confused, 'What's up with this flight?'

Turtles in shades, lounging on rocks,
Cracking jokes while avoiding the flocks.
The ocean's a stage, its performers shine,
Every creature proudly claims, 'This joke is mine!'

The breeze shares whispers, tickling the waves,
While shells tell tales of jovial knaves.
In this zany dance of earth and blue,
Laughter arises, 'What else is new?'

So let's raise our hats to the horizon vast,
Where giggles echo from futures cast.
As the sea meets sky, let joy take flight,
In this funny tale of day and night!

Voyager's Creed

To sail with joy and laugh at the tide,
To pretend the gulls join a dance by my side.
With a pop of my sail and a twist of my cap,
Every mishap is a fresh belly flap!

Navigating hiccups on a creaky old boat,
Whipping up soup from a sardine's coat.
The compass spins wildly, it knows not my way,
But I still hum and joke, come what may!

The ocean's a prankster, today it's a fool,
I'm the captain of goofs at this nautical school.
With each rolling wave, my spirit is free,
In the album of mishaps, I'm the VIP!

So here's to the sails that catch the wind's laugh,
And to all the trips down this soggy path.
With a wink and a grin, we'll embrace the ride,
As voyagers of fun, let's laugh side by side!

The Call of Distant Shores

A call from afar where the sand hugs the sea,
Echoes of laughter, come sail with me!
With flip-flops squeaking and sun hats askew,
Every adventure feels fresh and new.

The jellyfish dance, they're wobbly and free,
While the dolphins giggle, 'What about me?'
From coconut drinks to parrot squawks,
Life's a parade of outrageous talks!

Each shoreline whispers secrets untold,
Of sunburned noses and treasures of gold.
While sand between toes leads to glorious glee,
'Watch out for crabs! They're plotting,' says he.

So let's heed the call of those distant shores,
Where silliness roams and adventure soars.
In the carnival of currents, we'll dance around,
With laughter our anchor, let joy be unbound!

Flowing with Time

Tick-tock says the clock, oh what a tease,
Like a cat that prances, doing as it please.
I chase my dreams on roller skates,
While time just laughs and contemplates.

Trips to the fridge are my grandest quests,
Searching for snacks, I'm truly blessed.
But each time I snack, those minutes flee,
And I wonder if ice cream counts as a degree.

Yet I juggle chores like a circus clown,
With laundry balancing, I'm about to drown.
And when I finally sit down to unwind,
I trip on the dog, oh what a grind!

So here I am, with my bowl of cheer,
Flowing with time, raising a beer.
I toast to the chaos, the comedy divine,
For in this circus, I'm feeling just fine.

The Dance of Water and Stone

A river waltzes, skipping over pebbles,
While stones just sit, with their serious rebels.
They grumble and mumble, sitting with pride,
"Oh look at that water, it's 'flowing' worldwide!"

The rocks just stare, their expressions quite bland,
As the water swirls, like it's in a band.
"Hey, would you like to join us for a spin?"
"Oh no thank you, we're perfectly grim."

But then comes a flood, the stones start to shake,
"Okay, we'll dance, for goodness' sake!"
They wobble and bobble, in muddy delight,
As water keeps laughing, "What a silly sight!"

When the tide rolls back, they're stuck in a groove,
The dance of water and stone, with no need to prove.
In their watery ballet, both happy and free,
Who knew rocks could groove? Just you wait and see!

Sailing Beyond the Shores

A boat sets sail, with a clumsy cheer,
As I forget snacks, I've lost my dear.
The ocean giggles, swaying to its song,
While I question, "Did I pack enough for long?"

Seagulls dive-bomb, plotting a scheme,
"Is that your sandwich or part of a dream?"
I swat and I laugh 'til I spill my drink,
Oh, sailing's a hassle, but who has to think?

The captain's a cat, named Sir Fluff-a-lot,
He's steering us bigger, or so I thought.
With every wave that rocks the boat,
I wonder if it's me who needs to float!

As I navigate life with a giggle and grin,
I find every failure leads to new wins.
So here's to the journey, let's sail once more,
Beyond all the shores where the laughter can soar!

Reflections in the Tide

The ocean reflects all my silly blunders,
Like that time I danced and forgot my thunders.
I tripped on a jellyfish, joined in its show,
Now we'll be pals, forever aglow.

Each splash brings a joke, each ripple a grin,
While the tide plays tag, we all join in.
"Watch out for pirates!" my friends call to me,
But they're munching on chips, hardly a spree.

The shore writes my stories, each print a delight,
Of flips, flops, and falls that last into night.
With each breaking wave, I laugh in surprise,
At the fun in my journey, the joy in the skies!

So as the sun sets, and day turns to night,
I wave to the tide, "You've been such a delight!"
With memories of laughter, I'll cherish afar,
For the ocean's reflections are my guiding star.

Uncharted Waters

In a boat made of cereal, I set sail,
Chasing seagulls with gusto, I laugh, not fail.
The compass spins wildly, what a delightful mess,
Navigating chaos, I just wear a dress.

The fish in the ocean are all wearing hats,
Playing poker while dodging those fat, flapping cats.
I slip on a puddle, down into the blue,
Splashing with jellyfish, saying, "What's wrong with you?"

Octopus baristas serve coffee on demand,
While dolphins on surfboards think they're rock band.
I'm lost in the giggles of the great salty sea,
Life's an odd adventure, come sail it with me.

With rubber duckies sailing, we'll dance on the tide,
Rafts made of marshmallows, come join the ride.
Each splash is a laugh, each hiccup a cheer,
And with every mishap, the best times are here.

Floating on Memories' Breeze

I sailed on a puffball caught up in the gust,
Collecting all the crumbs of my childhood trust.
Kites made of wishes, they combat the breeze,
Plucking at the strings of the tall, swaying trees.

Clouds in a conga line dance overhead,
While squirrels in shades make a path 'round my head.
A yo-yoing seagull steals fries from my grip,
As laughter makes ripples in our little trip.

My boat's a banana, yellow and bright,
Rowing through memories twinkling with light.
I fish for my thoughts in the deep, silly sea,
Caught a glimpse of a party—sure looks fun to me!

Floating on giggles, oh what a delight,
The breeze carries whispers of wrong and of right.
With each goofy twist that popped up like cheese,
I'm floored by the flavors of life's melty breeze.

Between the Tides

Amidst all the mischief, the tide pulls us near,
A whirlpool of chaos, a chortle, a cheer.
The beach ball's a whale, and we're sinking in sand,
Building castles of laughter while we act so grand.

Balloons bobbing gently, they plot our escape,
Laughing seagulls conspire in their curious shape.
Let's toss in the surf, take a plunge, or a dive,
Find joy in the muck—hey, that's where we thrive!

The tide's a wild DJ, and we're dancing afloat,
With flip-flops as anchors, we drift, never gloat.
What's that in the distance? A beach chair parade?
Oh no, it's our friends—that's a costume charade!

Between every giggle, confusion may reign,
But each twist of the current is a festival gain.
So let's splash through the foamy, the silly, the bright,
As laughter tides over, we'll conquer the night.

Sailing Through Shadows

In shadows of palm trees, I ship set for glee,
With parrot-shaped snacks, we sail chortling free.
The moon is a disco ball, lighting up our night,
In this funky sea, everything feels just right.

We ride on the backs of a merry whale's grin,
Surfing the silence where the giggles begin.
Glowing squids are our lanterns, lighting the way,
As shadows do jigs for an unexpected play.

The stars are our crew, holding spatulas wide,
Flipping pancakes on deck; they're the best kind of ride.
With jellyfish waltzing, they join in the fun,
Making shadows in skips, under the giggling sun.

So hoist up the sails, let the laughter ring out,
Through shadows and gales, that's what life's all about.
With a wink and a splatter, we explore like brave fools,
Sailing through laughter, we break all the rules.

Uncharted Dreams

In sights unseen, we stumble and play,
Through maps made of giggles, we dance and sway.
With every odd turn, we chuckle and cheer,
Who needs a GPS when we've got good beer?

Navigating life is a hilarious ride,
With jellyfish flops and seagull pride.
We're lost in the funny, the bizarre, the grand,
Each detour a joke of a thwarted plan.

From sandy mishaps, to sunscreen slip-ups,
We toast to the chaos in plastic cup cups.
Adventure awaits, and it's all just a jest,
With laughter our compass, we're truly blessed.

So here's to the folly, the art of the roam,
In this quirky old world, we've crafted our home.
To uncharted dreams and the stories we tell,
We dive in headfirst with laughter to sell.

The Rhythm of the Coast

The tides reach for sand in a waltz so grand,
While crabs play the drums on the warm golden land.
Seagulls are singing, they've lost their cool,
As they steal fries like they rule the whole school.

Flip-flops are flapping, a rhythm on point,
We dance with the breeze while we snack at the joint.
The surf rolls in with a sassy flair,
And starfish go grooving with no need for care.

Shells tell a story of sandcastle fights,
Of battles with waves under starry night sights.
We're corny, we're silly, like kids from the block,
In this rhythm of laughter, we're free as a flock.

With each crashing wave, a tickle of fate,
We giggle at sea, till the hour gets late.
So raise up your toes to the beat and the fun,
In the dance of the coast, we are never outdone.

Serene Horizons

Up on the shore, where the calm seas lie,
The sun turns to laughter as gulls fly high.
In dreams dressed in bubbles, we float and we beam,
With jellyfish giggles, it's all just a dream.

Beneath the bright skies, the piers sway and creak,
Where fishermen's tales turn to comedic streaks.
With rods turned to rascals and nets filled with glee,
They'll barter with fish—"Just look at that spree!"

Horizons so vast, where the humor does glide,
In jokes made of sunshine and smiles, we abide.
With every horizon, new chuckles arise,
In the silence of sunsets, it's laughter that flies.

So here's to the calm and the silliness found,
In the space where the ocean and laughter abound.
As the horizon winks with a whimsical spin,
We roll with the joy, let the antics begin.

Echoes of the Deep

In the depths below, the fish have a ball,
They jest with the seaweed and giggle so small.
With dolphins that dance and whales with a joke,
The deep is alive with its merry folks.

As tides pull and tug, the laughter will spread,
With conch shells snickering, "Don't wake the dead!"
The octopus juggles, a master of flair,
While crabs crack wise without a single care.

Each bubble a chuckle from creatures obscure,
With echoes of laughter, we find the allure.
For deep in these waters, the funny prevails,
Through frolicsome fishes and ridiculous gales.

So dive into the depths where humor will thrive,
In a world that's absurd, where the silly's alive.
With echoes of joy that will tickle your soul,
Life under the sea takes a humor-filled stroll.

Secrets in the Swell

In a sea of socks, where treasures hide,
Float rubber ducks, with no place to glide.
The crabs throw parties, on moonlit sand,
While I chase memories, things got out of hand.

Seagulls steal fries, as I laugh and shout,
My sunscreen bottle is empty, no doubt.
The ocean's a jester, it plays with my hair,
I dive for a shell and find a lost pair.

With waves that dance, tickling my toes,
I slip on a wave, fall right on my nose.
Fish giggle softly, swim circles around,
While the tide waves hello, I'm upside down!

So let's pack our troubles and swim far away,
Make friends with the dolphins, what do they say?
With laughter and splashes, we'll float and we'll bide,
In this sea of silliness, come take a ride!

Ebb and Flow

The tide pulled my sandwich, oh what a sight,
It vanished in seconds, now that's not polite.
As jellyfish waltz on this beach party scene,
I'm left with crumbs, if I could just glean!

With each ebbing giggle, I'm swept into glee,
As sea turtles paddle, just waiting for tea.
Fins flipping and flapping, they laugh with delight,
"Grab your surfboard, it's a swell of a night!"

I played a grand game of peek-a-boo sand,
With starfish applauding, can you understand?
The ocean's my jester, it tickles my heart,
As it ebbs and it flows, a whimsical art.

So raise your coconuts and cheer with a shout,
The ocean won't keep our laughter without!
In this rhythm of life, take a leap and joke,
With every wave's giggle, let's give it a poke!

Oceans of Memory

I built a grand castle, it stood just so tall,
But a sneaky old wave gave it quite the fall.
With buckets and shovels, we laugh and we play,
In the ocean's embrace, we're swept far away.

The crabs dressed in jackets, oh what a sight,
They strut on the sand, feeling fancy tonight.
Each splash is a chuckle, a wave of pure cheer,
As I tumble and giggle, drifting without fear.

In seas of nostalgia, the past likes to tease,
With seaweed as confetti, it's a party, if you please.
The dolphins remind me, with flips and with spins,
That laughter's the treasure, where the fun always begins.

So let's gather the shells, and tell tales galore,
Of the times that we puzzled and danced on the shore.
With oceans of memory, and tides that adore,
We're laughing through life, who could ask for more?

Merging with the Horizon

As the sun takes a dive, the sky paints a grin,
I search for my flip-flops, they're lost in the din.
With seagulls debating, do I join their squaw?
Or chase down the snacks that I just saw withdraw?

In the dance of the moments, I trip on the foam,
While shells plot a heist, they're calling it home.
The horizon's a mystery, with jokes in the mist,
I wave at the sunset, can you believe this?

With laughter as fuel, we surf on the breeze,
Dodging the jellyfish, and a pile of leaves.
The ocean's a canvas, my painting of fun,
As we blend into twilight, all worries undone.

So gather your friends, and let worries drift,
As the waves throw a party, in the evening's swift lift.
With smiles wide as the horizon, let's dance, don't delay,
For in this ocean of chuckles, we'll surf through the day!

Surges of Emotion

Bubbles burst with every cheer,
Giggles pop as we draw near.
Splashing in the puddles bright,
We chase the sun from morn to night.

Silly hats and rubber ducks,
We gather hope like goldenucks.
Riding high on laughter's crest,
In this hilarious quest, we're blessed.

Tumbling down like jolly clowns,
Sailing through our joyful towns.
With every flip and silly dance,
Life's absurd, but we take our chance.

From frowns to grins, we shift the scene,
Hiccups echo, where we've been.
Like juggling pies and dodging fate,
We embrace the laughs, it's never late.

Journeying Through the Mist

Fog rolls in on whispers sweet,
In the haze, we dance on feet.
Ducks and geese play peek-a-boo,
As we wander, treasuring the view.

Muddy paths with squishy shoes,
Finding treasures, sharing news.
With every turn, a twist awaits,
Unicorns, strawberries, funny mates!

Spinning stories that float like dreams,
In this mist, nothing's as it seems.
Embrace the goofs, the funny sights,
It's a silly ride through fuzzy lights.

Drift along, just let it be,
Laughter's compass sets us free.
In the blur, we find our song,
With giggles guiding us along.

Celestial Currents

Stars above, our guide tonight,
Tickling dreams with cosmic light.
Planets spin in joyful glee,
As fishing hooks catch fond esprit.

Floating by in disco balls,
Galaxies in silly stalls.
With rubber moons and bouncing suns,
We ride the highs like happy runs.

Jellybean comets zoom and dash,
In our rocket ship, we splash.
Funny faces in the stars,
Explorers of the absurd, not far.

So here we are; it's quite a show,
Cosmic laughs that freely flow.
Join the ride, let laughter reign,
In this vast space, we'll dance again.

The Dance of the Sea

Crabs in tuxedos waltz around,
Seashells laugh with a chatter sound.
The dolphins flip and make a splash,
While seagulls gossip, what a bash!

Flip-flops flying left and right,
In the sun, we dance with delight.
With each twirl, we trip and fall,
But hey, who cares? We're having a ball!

Seaweed sways in funny rhythm,
It's a rollercoaster of whimsy, a prism.
Jellyfish join in a conga line,
In this beach party, all things combine.

So grab your friends, let's make a scene,
In this ocean's dance, we're all serene.
We chase the tide, we set it free,
Life's a dance, come join the spree!

Currents of Yesterday

The tide brought back my old flip-flops,
With holes so big, they could hold my crops.
I tried to wear them, but oh what a sight,
Great for the beach, but not for a night!

The seagulls laughed as they stole my fries,
I thought they were friends, oh what a surprise!
Now I'm in a race, trying to reclaim,
My lunch from those birds - it's a seagull game!

The beach ball bounced, a twist of fate,
Hit a kid hard; he wasn't too late.
He chased it down, slipped on the sand,
Dance like a fish? Oh, he had it planned!

But each chase led to giggles, bright grins,
Life's funny moments, where joy always wins.
For every misstep, there's laughter to find,
Currents of yesterday, life's playful grind.

The Nature of Movement

At dawn, I tried to jog, oh what a scene,
Tripped on my shoelace like I was a teen.
The neighbor laughed, said, "You've got your charm!"
I waved and fell; guess it's my own alarm!

The wind whispered tales, chased leaves on the run,
It tickled a dog; now they're having fun!
He chased a squirrel, oh what a delight,
Nature's a comic, a pure sheer respite!

I danced with the tides, the moon gave a wink,
Lost my balance! Who needs a drink?
Bubbles around me, laughter ensues,
Life's nature of movement, it's all just a cruise!

So here's to the slip-ups, the chuckles we share,
Life's little follies, we should all be aware.
In motion, we find joy, let's groove and spin,
The laughter keeps coming, let the fun begin!

Ripple Effect

Dropped a pebble, watched it spin wide,
My dog jumped in; oh, what a ride!
He splashed all around, soaked my old shoes,
I laughed till I cried; what does one do?

The ducks quacked loudly, giving me sass,
Didn't know they were holding a class!
"Fetch!", one yelled, "You're doing it wrong!"
"Just make me a snack," with a much sassier song!

The ripples spread laughter, silly and bright,
Each splash was a giggle, in morning light.
My coffee spilled too, but who really cares?
The mess is just part of life's funny affairs!

With each little ripple, joy keeps afloat,
A game of surprises, a quacking note.
In puddles of laughter, we find our wit,
Such is the ripple, life's comedy bit!

Spirit of the Ocean

The ocean sings softly, a salty old tale,
Of fish in bow ties caught in the gale.
They wiggle and giggle, regale every seal,
"Dress like a shrimp? That's just surreal!"

A crab in a tux, quite stylish and neat,
"Gala tonight? No!" He danced on the beat.
The jellyfish glowed, a disco so bright,
Moving like dancers in the deep of the night!

Then came the waves, with a knock and a roll,
Spilling my ice cream; that's taking a toll!
But laughter erupted, the summer so sweet,
Even the seagulls joined in for a treat!

So here's to the spirit, the fun and the cheer,
Dance with the ocean, let go of the fear.
For life's just a party, in sun or in rain,
Embrace every moment; let happiness reign!

Embracing Transience

Life's a beach, with grains of sand,
We build our castles, not quite as planned.
The tide pulls away, our dreams in a swirl,
Gotta laugh as they crash, what a crazy world!

Seagulls steal fries, and joy's on the run,
We chase after sunsets, thinking we're done.
But moments like jellyfish, float in the air,
Swim with the fishes, if you double the dare!

Now here comes the tide, with a splash and a cheer,
We surf on our worries, no need for a fear.
So take out your boogie board, join in the fun,
Life's a quirky ride, we never outrun!

With laughter and bubbles, let's dance in the spray,
In this watery journey, we splash and we play.
Embrace every ripple, let your heart sing,
For life's like a tide, and joy is the king!

Beyond the Calm

In still waters, I fish for my muse,
Caught a shoe instead, now that's the news!
The tranquil scene's teeming with quirks galore,
While ducks quack in harmony, demanding encore.

A picnic planned perfectly, just down the creek,
Only to find ants had taken a peek.
They marched off with crumbs like a marching band,
Life's little surprises—too funny to stand!

Skimming stones, oh what a sport,
Each one a misfire, a comic retort.
But laughter erupts when the splash goes wide,
Who knew stone-throwing could fill us with pride?

With a wink at the clouds, I'm ready to play,
The funny side of troubles just lights up the day.
In jest and in joy, I embrace what's ahead,
For what's truly funny is the path we once tread!

Shoreline Stories

Gather 'round, let me spin you a tale,
Of crabs in tuxedos, swaying like a whale.
On the shoreline, the seagulls rehearsed,
Their pirate accents, oh how they burst!

Sandcastles crumble like dreams in the night,
As kids giggle, taking flight in delight.
Each grain of sand whispers secrets untold,
Of mermaids who sunbathe with treasures of gold.

Beachballs and boogie boards, sunburned and sweet,
The surf tells a joke as it laughs at our feet.
Chasing after the tide, we slip and we slide,
What a world of laughter we can't help but ride!

So grab your flip-flops, don't miss the fun,
The shoreline is jokester, always on the run.
With every sweet moment, a joyful score,
Life's a shoreline party, who could ask for more?

Awakening the Depths

Under the surface, where fish like to hide,
A mermaid's lost earring, a real goofy ride.
They say to dive deep, it's all in your head,
But watch out for octopus, they're mischief bred!

Bubbles erupt like laughter from below,
Each burst a reminder of the joy we bestow.
Treasure maps drawn with crayon and cheer,
Discovering giggles, no need to fear!

The calm of the ocean may make you feel sad,
Till dolphins arrive, playing tricks that make you glad.
Flip upside down, in a whirl of delight,
Let the rhythm of water power your flight!

So take the plunge, with a cannonball twist,
Each splash is a chance, you just can't resist.
For the depths of existence hold stories so bright,
Let's awaken the magic, from morning to night!

Lost in the Drift

I lost my hat in the ocean's dance,
It twirled and spun, a carefree prance.
I chased it down with a playful shout,
But the seagulls laughed as they flapped about.

The tides are tricky, they pull and tease,
I drift along with the jellyfish breeze.
They wave their tentacles, so full of glee,
While I just hope they won't notice me.

The sand gets stuck in places quite weird,
My flip-flops squeak, oh how they've steered!
Each step a comedy, trip and fall,
The shoreline giggles, it's a free-for-all.

I build a castle, it teeters and leans,
Just like my life, filled with laughs and scenes.
As the tide rolls in, my structure will flop,
But who needs walls when you've got a soft drop?

Tracing the Shoreline

Walking the beach, it's a wobbly stroll,
My toes in the sand, my mind's in a hole.
I dig for treasures, but find only shells,
That whisper secrets and ocean spells.

Squirrels in swimsuits dart by the sea,
Chasing each other, as silly as can be.
With every splash, they squeal in delight,
While I laugh hard — what a goofy sight!

Sunburned folks in bright-colored gear,
Dance like crabs, and it's perfectly clear.
Who knew a sun hat could look so bizarre?
I'd trade mine for humor, don't care who you are!

In the distance, a dog steals a snack,
As its owner yells, "Oh, bring my chips back!"
Life's little moments, all silly and small,
Turn a stroll on the beach into the best of them all.

Celestial Navigation

I'm lost at sea, but not really mad,
With a map that's scribbly, how can I be bad?
I use the stars as my guide tonight,
But they're all winking, what a funny sight!

The moon's a big cheese, I swear it's true,
I tried to take a bite, but it dodged me too.
Constellations giggle as I float along,
With fish throwing parties in a school so strong.

A dolphin swims by, plays peek-a-boo,
Winking at me like it already knew.
I try to follow, but it dances ahead,
With a flick of its tail, it's off like a thread.

Navigating life with a whimsical flair,
Each detour taken leads me somewhere rare.
As I drift among stars, I laugh with delight,
Life's a comic strip wrapped in the night.

In the Embrace of the Ocean

Tangled in seaweed, what a delightful mess,
I'm here for a swim, not a floral dress.
The ocean wraps 'round with a giggle and cheer,
It whispers, "Stay close, you belong here!"

Splashing like whales, we dance in the foam,
My dog thinks he's a shark; this is his home.
He lunges for bubbles, and I just can't cope,
With laughter erupting, he's my splashy hope.

The gulls dive down, with a hoot and a flap,
"Hey there, two-legged, don't you take a nap!"
Each break and cackle, a reminder to play,
As I float in bliss while the sun fades away.

In deep waters, wisdom gets lost in the fun,
With every splash, we melt into one.
A world full of antics, both salty and sweet,
In the embrace of the ocean, I find my beat.

Tides of Change

The tide rolls in with a giggle,
Seagulls dance, making us wiggle.
A boat flips over, what a sight!
Splash! A swimmer takes flight.

The sandcastle stands, but not for long,
A wave crashes down, what a song!
Buckets and shovels, all askew,
A toddler's grin, what can we do?

The beach ball sails through the air,
A game of dodge, without a care.
Laughter echoes, the sun shines bright,
Losing the match? It feels just right!

Flip-flops fly as we run, oh dear,
Sand in our toes, it tickles, we cheer!
With every splash, we lose our frown,
In every dip, we wear our crown!

The Rhythm of Progression

The clock ticks on, what a beat,
To dance in circles, oh so sweet.
Missed deadlines? Let's have a laugh,
Delay? Find joy in the gaffe!

Through ups and downs, we leap and twirl,
Life's a dance, give it a whirl.
Spinning in circles, we trip and tease,
Losing our focus, but who cares, please!

The rhythm stumbles, we join in fun,
Every misstep, we pardon one.
High fives and giggles, we celebrate,
With each little blunder, we elevate!

So, let's sway to this wild tune,
Under the stars or the sun at noon.
Life's a party, don't miss a beat,
Dance like nobody's got two left feet!

Currents of Time

A clock that tick-tocks like a game,
Chasing after minutes, what a shame!
Lost in the flow, we giggle and sigh,
Who knew time flies with every pie?

Rushing to catch each fleeting hour,
With coffee in hand, we seek the power.
Emails and tasks, like fish they swim,
Still, we make time for a little whim!

Tickle a friend, make them snort,
For laughter's the best, a joyful sport.
In the current's grip, we shake and jest,
Time's elusive, but we're truly blessed!

So here's to moments we can't rewind,
With giggles and gags, we're intertwined.
Time's a river, flowing fast and wide,
Let's float along, with hearts open wide!

Echoes of the Ocean's Heart

Hear the waves, they're whispering tales,
Of fish in tuxedos and lobster gales.
Shells that giggle as they roll on sand,
A crab in a top hat, isn't life grand?

The ocean's laughter bubbles and sings,
A chorus of joy, oh what joy it brings!
With seashells clinking, like glasses toast,
To those silly dolphins, we love the most!

A tidepool party, sea stars in lines,
Their dance is quirky, a sight so fine!
They wobble and giggle, a funny spoof,
In this underwater ballroom, we're all goof!

So listen closely to the soft ocean hum,
It carries our laughter, it keeps us young.
With each splash and swirl, we find our place,
In echoes of joy, we embrace the grace!

Drifting Through Reflections

I met a fish who wore a hat,
He asked me where the snacks were at.
I said, "Just follow the bread crumbs,
We'll catch a meal until it comes!"

A turtle winked with a cheeky grin,
"Life's a game; let's spin and spin!"
We drifted past a dancing whale,
Who told us jokes about a sail!

We laughed so hard, we forgot the route,
A seagull squawked, "What's that about?"
"We're lost, but hey, let's grab a bite,
This underwater world feels just right!"

So here we float with laughs galore,
Sharing puns, who could ask for more?
With salty laughs and fishy cheer,
Our quirky journey has no fear!

The Flow of Memories

A jellyfish once made a pie,
With gooey filling, oh my, oh my!
I tried a slice, it did a dance,
Then wobbled off to join a prance!

A clam declared, "Let's throw a ball!"
The crab DJ was quite a call.
With funky moves beneath the sea,
We bubbled up with glee, just free!

Old octopus showed off his moves,
While laughing, he improved the grooves.
Each pop and twist made memories,
Flowing like a swarm of bees!

In swirling tides of blissful jest,
We played until the sun would rest.
Our silly songs will never fade,
In deep blue, we've truly played!

Ripples of Experience

The goldfish wore a tiny shirt,
While searching for his lost dessert.
"Have you seen my cake?" he cried,
As minnows giggled, trying to hide.

We built a castle made of sand,
But then the tide had other plans.
A crab proclaimed, "We need a moat!"
I said, "Let's build on a bigger float!"

A dolphin swam by, full of cheer,
"Forget the castle, let's go steer!"
With laughter bubbling all around,
Our adventure kept growing sound!

So here we are, a merry crew,
Making ripples with things we do.
From silly pranks to tasty treats,
Life's a splash, just funny feats!

Navigating the Depths

A shark in specs read a map,
He said, "This route's quite the trap!"
So we took a detour through the mud,
Where sea cucumbers laughed in a thud.

We met a squid who played the flute,
With a tentacle dance that was absolute!
Anemones swayed, feeling the beat,
As we all gathered, moving our feet!

"This way's better, no need to pout,
Just follow me; I know the route!"
But then we tripped on a school of fish,
And wished for a nice, calm little dish.

With bubbles floating, we made a cheer,
Navigating with laughter, never fear!
For in the depths, we found our way,
Turning troubles into a bright ballet!

The Lighthouse of Tomorrow

Standing tall on rocks of dreams,
A beacon made of ice cream scoops.
It guides the boats with silly beams,
While seagulls laugh in funny loops.

With jellyfish in polka dots,
And crabs that dance the cha-cha slide,
This lighthouse knows all the right spots,
Where wishes and giggles do collide.

So if you're lost, no need to fret,
Just follow the scent of bubble gum.
The lighthouse beams a full-on duet,
Where laughter's the key and fun's the sum.

In the night, it shines and glows,
With disco balls and silly tunes.
Bright colors burst and laughter flows,
As night's heroes float like balloons.

A Symphony of Horizons

In the orchestra of sunny days,
Trombones slide with ice cream sprinkles.
The sun's a trumpet in funny ways,
As clouds do tap dance with soft twinkles.

With each wave comes a new refrain,
The surfboard choir sings a song.
A symphony that's never plain,
With melodies that chirp along.

Seashells play a maraca beat,
While starfish twirl on sandy shores.
This concert's not for the elite,
It's for those who laugh and explore.

From the east to the western skies,
The harmony of joy is cast.
Waves of chuckles gently rise,
In this grand show, we're all amassed.

The Call of Distant Shores

A parrot squawks, its feathers bright,
On distant shores where giggles bloom.
It calls out loud with all its might,
As beach balls bounce and kites consume.

With flip-flops slapping at the sand,
Adventures waiting, oh so bold.
The crabs in costumes take a stand,
While tales of fun are joyfully told.

Tropical drinks with silly straws,
Bring laughter to the sun-kissed crew.
Each shore a land without a cause,
Where jellybeans and dreams come true.

So heed the call, embrace the thrill,
With sandy feet and spirits light.
Let laughter linger, joy fulfill,
In this paradise of pure delight.

Transitions in the Breeze

The wind whispers secrets all around,
It tickles leaves with silly cheer.
In every gust, a playful sound,
As butterflies dance near and dear.

From one season to the next we glide,
With socks that don't quite match our shoes.
In every twist, we take in stride,
With laughter as our easy muse.

A leaf orchestra plays a show,
As squirrels wear hats while they prance.
This dance of change will surely grow,
As giggles join in the lively chance.

So let the breeze take us away,
In silly hats and playful glee.
Embrace the fun in every sway,
In transitions, we find the key.

Under the Celestial Sea

Under the stars that twinkle bright,
I tripped on a crab in the pale moonlight.
The fish laughed hard, or so it seemed,
As I danced like a fool, or maybe dreamed.

With jellyfish gliding, I tried to impress,
But tangled my feet in a slippery mess.
Seashells chuckled, they knew my fate,
As I wobbled and giggled, oh isn't life great?

A dolphin swam by, gave me a glance,
I waved like a mermaid, made quite a stance.
The tide rolled in, with a splash and a cheer,
I'd swear I heard ocean giggles, quite clear.

So here's to the deep, with its quirky charm,
Where every misstep will cause a alarm.
Let's dive with joy, catch the fish of delight,
And dance with the sea under the starry night.

Turning Tides

In the morning sun, the seafoam winks,
As I ponder my life over cool kitchen drinks.
The seagulls squawk, with opinions to share,
About my beach hat, or lack of hair.

Sailing along, in a boat made of hopes,
I swore I saw dolphins, or were they just soaps?
With every tide, my snacks took a dive,
And my balance was gone, how could I survive?

But laughter is salt, that flavors the fight,
As I belly flop straight into the light.
With sardines applauding from a can on the shore,
I laugh to myself, as I swim back for more.

So let the tide turn, let chaos unfold,
With a surfboard of dreams, we'll be fearless and bold.
For life's but a splash, a tickle, a tease,
And who doesn't laugh at the whims of the breeze?

The Salt of Experience

In a world where fish wear tiny hats,
And sea cucumbers do acrobatic chats,
I've learned from the crabs, with their sidestepping grace,
That living is better with sand in your face.

Each grain's a story, each wave sings a tune,
With clams playing guitar beneath the bright moon.
I slipped on a shell, did the twist and the shout,
And even the barnacles laughed all about.

A wise octopus tells jokes with a wink,
While I ponder if seaweed can help me think.
The turtles just nod, with their zen kind of style,
As I roll in the surf, dazzled by their guile.

So here's my mantra, all sticky and sweet,
With salt in the air, and sand on my feet.
Experience glimmers through laughter and cheer,
Making every moment a treasure sincere.

Infinite Ripples

I tossed a pebble, watched the ripples unfurl,
And giggled at the fish chasing after a swirl.
They bumped into each other, what a fine show,
A water ballet with nowhere to go.

The tide brought a message, all splashes and grins,
An invitation for barnacles with shoes full of pins.
I joined their parade, we marched to the beat,
Turning clams into tambourines, oh what a feat!

Around me, the ocean was buzzing with fun,
As crabs played charades, and the dolphin would run.
Each ripple a giggle, an echo of play,
In the vast, endless sea, come join our buffet.

So here's to the ripples, both small and grand,
That tickle our toes and offer a hand.
Let life be a splash, with laughter as bait,
In this ocean of joy, let's celebrate fate!

www.ingramcontent.com/pod-product-compliance
Lightning Source LLC
Chambersburg PA
CBHW062112280426
43661CB00086B/559